LINES IN OPPOSITION

MAUREEN SHERBONDY

LINES IN OPPOSITION
Copyright © 2022 Maureen Sherbondy
All Rights Reserved.
Published by Unsolicited Press.
Printed in the United States of America.
First Edition.

No part of this book may be used or reproduced in any manner whatsoever without written permission except in the case of brief quotations embodied in critical articles or reviews.

Attention schools and businesses: for discounted copies on large orders, please contact the publisher directly.

For information contact:
Unsolicited Press
Portland, Oregon
www.unsolicitedpress.com
orders@unsolicitedpress.com
619-354-8005

Cover Design: Kathryn Gerhardt
Editor: Bekah Stogner

ISBN: 978-1-956692-10-5

ACKNOWLEDGMENTS

"Erase" appeared in *January Review*

"Fire Sale, Baby" and "My Neighbor Cleans Up Crime Scenes" appeared in *The Lake*

"Gretel" appeared in *Pinesongs*

"Line" appeared in *Freshwater*

"Line Dancers" appeared in *Halcyone*

"My Father Returns from New York City" appeared in *The Lascaux Review*

"Sparring at the Party of the Literati" appeared in *Amethyst*

"Synthesis" and "The Drowned Boy" appeared in *Kakalak*

"Transitions" appeared in *The Broad River Review*

Poems

LINES   11
   Sparring at the Party of the Literati   12
   Line   13
   Gretel   15
   Ash Tales   18
   Leaving Ashbery Behind   19
   Transitions   20
   Seagull   22
   Erase   24
   Stripes   25
   Listen   27
   Stairway to Heaven   28
   Hurricane Lover   30
   The Patio   31
   The Defiant Poet   33
   A Plot   34
   Synthesis   35
   Square   37
   Scales, an Abecedarian Poem   38
   Splatter   40
   Line Dancers   41

Indecisive	42
Aisle	44
Grocery Lines	45
Basho, Spring, and My Shadow	47
Why Worry	48

OPPOSITION — 49

Fire Sale, Baby	50
Terrible Dictators	52
The Arbitration	53
Making My Students Cry in Class	54
The Squirrel Trapped in the Ceiling of the Adjunct Office	56
It's Good to Get Lost	58
Bend	59
Casting Away Sins	61
Meteorology	62
When the Devil Comes Knocking	64
Reveal	66
Migraines Ashore in Florida	68
Food Fight at Walmart	70
Curmudgeons	71
Circle on Canvas	72
The Angry Son Grows Up	73

Folly	74
The Ant	75
Education	77
TALES FROM THE CITY	79
My Father Returns from New York City	80
At 6 AM You Still Speak with Your Father	82
God Whispers	83
Jazz Club Limbo	84
Gate	87
Happy Hour	88
Barstool Time	90
Change of Address	91
Smoke	92
Those Who Do Sickness	94
My Neighbor Cleans Up Crime Scenes	96
Bubble Yum Urban Myth	97
Lips	98
The Worker	100
Wealthy People	101
At the Greyhound Bus Station, Nashville	102

For Barry Peters

LINES IN OPPOSITION

Lines

Sparring at the Party of the Literati

Always the fate question waiting
on acquaintances' lips at the party
of literate friends and erudite foes in the city
row house while the host serves plates
of ceviche, roe, and pâté. Two guests arrive
late, then proceed to obliterate
the conversation *in medias res*. Spectators
all of us, Godot-esque, we wait for
the boxing match to begin and end
with one determination—free will or fate,
the sated winner holding one victorious
boxing glove while the other hand hesitates.

Line

The line leads to nowhere,
unless you count
the roller-coaster or spinning
teacups as somewhere.

If you draw a line in the sand,
some Northerner will likely
lunge past it, fists flailing
everywhere and nowhere.

A room you once entered
at nineteen contained
a line of boy-men eager
to snort cocaine
up aquiline snouts
so they could forget.

One winter in below-zero temperature,
you waited at a New York theatre
to take a seat and witness

a line of Rockettes kicking
up feet, wanting to dance
beyond the audience and staged air.

The line of trees is deceptive
for the woman trying to pass through
a single layer; instead, she finds herself
wandering, lost inside an entire forest.

Gretel

You can no longer follow
the crumbs back home;
the crows and blackbirds
grew starved over the years.

Can you blame hunger
for wiping clean the past?
Home is never the place
you remember, anyway.

The bi-level house has been
shrunken. Those rosebushes
planted with your drunken father
were ripped out. The neighbors

relocated to nursing homes
or rest now in boxes
set deep inside the earth.
New children play catch

in the street. A different dog
barks at night. Around the curve,

another father is punching holes
into walls with his angry fist.

        *

It is long past curfew.
Do not ask how
to arrive back home
without notice.

Do not ask where
the siblings went
in the spent hours
beyond dusk.

You have forgotten
to return after years
away. There were dances
and games, meandering travels.

Here, the dog no longer
barks in the yard
and the songbird
on the sill has gone silent.

Now you set older fists
against the familiar red door,
but only ghosts wait upstairs
inside your parents' bed.

Ash Tales

Yesterday, the ash line appeared
on the grass. Do you remember
when you called from the porch,
pining for words? You said,
Tell me a story.

My feet are now coated
in gray. Soot rests on my face.
I raced through fires
for you, darling, stepping
on burnt ground and black weeds.

Fire lines scarring my skin show
what happens when one doesn't
let go of pain. My story was
about a woman who tried
to run away from the house.

Not that story, you said.
I can't help it. Truth
is the only gift I can give.

Leaving Ashbery Behind

I left you on my cold desk
in an office where a woman
listened to sexual harassment
videos while Spanish students
paraded in and out muttering in
broken English. They ignored you,
then stole chocolate bars
from the bowl beside your cover.
I left you in a diner
where your spine absorbed
the scent of pastrami on rye,
until you choked on
a heavy dose of chlorine at the Y.
In bed I dreamed of convex mirrors
and distorted lines and faces.
By morning, I wished I could
comprehend your vague abstractions
and all those insightful stanzas.

Transitions

I never learned them either. Thoughts ricochet
from ceiling to floor, from grocery lists
to doctor appointments. My mother skips
from conversation about atrial fibrillation
to the Atlantic City bus trip in a microsecond.
Maybe the sudden departure from Germany to America
was to blame for her inability to make use of them.

In my home state of New Jersey, no signals
are used when shifting from lane to lane;
letting drivers know the plan only leads to cut-offs
and brake-slamming. And did you hear about
the Vegas shooter? No lovely transition to the other side
exists for-bullet-in-the head sudden ends. They were
listening to music one moment, dead the next.

Men in my family die suddenly,
no chance for hospice care or slow final days
for last goodbyes. My father flatlined
in a second when his heart stopped.
My grandfather's artery burst; he flew
away without a departing utterance.

In school, my English teacher discussed building
bridges between paragraphs. I was home with bronchitis.
Life is not seamless. Like bad carnival rides, subjects
jerk from one track to the next. Even my own birth
jumped the transition phase, labor proceeding directly to
       pushing.

My father left abruptly without a sit-down with us children;
divorce came like a tornado, arriving without warning.
I would have made a terrible deejay, no common chords
between tunes, spinning Talking Heads, then Air Supply.
Put words on a wall, hope they stick. I am trying to make
       sense
of a world that throws rocks without a signal phrase or a
       single warning.

Seagull

We found the drowned boy at dusk,
his bloated body drifting ashore
wrapped in seaweed. Facedown,
he landed at our feet.

Meg thought she felt a jellyfish,
but her scream that filled
the gritty air said otherwise.

He'd been missing three days.
While he walked, a wave
strong-armed him away
to sea never to be seen again.

There is no God, cried Meg,
pulling her foot back as if burned
by the carcass. I dragged the weight

from foamy water and sat
in sand as if waiting for

an answer to dive from the sky.
Instead, a seagull landed
beside me, his sharp beak
expectant, waiting.

Erase

We have erased the others,
those men, those women
who came before us,
the smeared kisses
in hallways, the neck nibbles
in cars, the barroom tiffs
and alley seductions.

I has shifted to *we*
like that old house
where the owner bulldozed
all interior walls
to create one giant room
of us.

Stripes

Pull stripes from the garden,
then sew them into magic fabric
in petals of yellow and purple.
Line a cloth path to that place
you left behind at nine years old.

Staring at that sombrero provides
no answers. Bolero-dance away
from what you have always feared.
Beneath the bed are dusty secrets
and fuzzy slippers. The only
monsters ever witnessed
lived in your parents' bed.

Once, a lit starfish flew from the sky
and landed inside your room;
you still doubt seeing what
resides right in front of you.

At the edge of your yard,
a bottle holds final answers
on a thin strip of paper.

Even now, you are afraid
to remove that cork
and measure the truth.

Listen

To the winning numbers spinning
inside your ears as the croupier
twirls the roulette wheel around again.

To the long-dead voices
of your ancestors rumbling when warm
leaves shake in the cold winter wind
to guide you to the where and when.

To the inside-the-head Muses
pleading, *Wait, just wait,*
seconds before the truck
speeds through that red light.

Stairway to Heaven

They said "Stairway to Heaven" played
backwards becomes a prayer to Satan.
I didn't know what a prayer to Satan
sounded like. Would there be yelling
and chalkboard screeching? A promise
to visit in the afterlife? All I knew
about the devil I learned watching
Rosemary's Baby and *The Exorcist*.
I was unsure why anyone would
pray to an evil creature. Was this
a clandestine code as in spy movies
when top secret messages appear
in foreign newspaper classified ads?
There was such uncertainty related
to this entire prayer phenomenon.
In fact, I wasn't sure what a prayer
even was. Praying occurred in temple,
Hebrew blessings to Adonai. Bending
and bowing. And silent prayer, where
stillness entered the shul. Here I noticed
the backs of men's and women's heads adorned
with blue and black kippahs or white, lacy coverings.

Prayers to Satan only led to nightmares. At fourteen
when I danced with a boy shorter
than me, I pictured fire and sulfur
racing through the middle school cafeteria
as soon as the deejay played that famous song.

Hurricane Lover

You tease me for ten days
whipping around the shifting
dance floor, twisting and turning
toward smaller, thinner bodies.

I wait for you, prepare
my water and wine supply,
stock up, ready for your arrival.

Honey, you finally come
howling in dancing circles,
moving every object in your path,
slamming into me head-on.

Then I am left wet and bereft.
You are gone, leaving disaster
and my broken self behind.

The Patio

The making of the patio is progressing
rather slowly. Workers set a frame too small
and low to satisfy the size requirements
clearly stated in the builder's contract.

I watch the new-poured rectangle with growing
animosity. Sludge flows forth like batter,
dries and solidifies. Then I notify
the man in charge of men,
wondering if the workers
interpreted twelve as two instead. They ought
to learn to measure properly.

Three times now, they've ripped up
the shape, dragged away the corpse
of shame, error of cracked cake,
then left behind a muddy mess
for the neighborhood to witness
this construction digression.

Torn grass and so much ragged earth
exist in this war zone of incompetence.

The making of the patio is turning
into quite a show, while profit
for the man deteriorates with every new mistake.
The next time they attempt another crass
rebuild, I'll leave keepsakes in the yard,
so in the end, the patio turns out right
with my gift of measuring tape and glasses.

The Defiant Poet

Like a rebellious teenager, her poems
exist in opposition, refuse to be orderly
and upright neatly beside neighboring poems.
Folded accordion instead, like a map
to be pulled out and studied.

Indecipherable for the sake of obscurity.
I try to locate a dot on the map, to discover
structure by following nouns and verbs
to see if one road leads to another.

But always I end up lost
in alphabet slums, asking how and why
I am even here, left
worn and dirty at the end of the line.

A Plot

It was about
a man and a woman
falling in love.
No, it was about
a man and a woman divorcing
and a son who ran from home
to join the circus or the army
or the sales force at Cisco.
There was a death, a funeral,
a wedding. Things happened.
People settled on a plot
of land. Holes were dug,
someone fell in. A fire came
and burned away the story.

Synthesis

I say, *Find the threads
between the articles.*
My students stare blankly,
do not know what I mean.

It's not their fault –
they are eighteen, nineteen, twenty-two.
I see them between classes
rushing through the halls,

faces stuck between loss
and phone screens, eyes scanning
photos, Facebook feeds, texts.
Read each article first, I instruct.

Annotate. They complain that
it's too long an assignment,
too hard, too late. Couldn't they see
a movie instead? They murmur.

The topic is poverty, I add.
They nod. Each student is filling

a seat in this community college.
Their wages won't pay higher rates.

One boy wears holey jeans;
four students missed the last paper
because they work two jobs.
The threads of their shirts

and pants are hanging from wear.
Find the thread, I repeat.
Absentmindedly, one student
pulls at a dangling red thread

and the entire shirt threatens to unravel.

Square

Let's not fight.
Why not see it
from my angle?
All sides are equal.

Why must there be
sides at all?
One likes to think
outside the square.

If you don't stand
beyond the box,
when the fire burns,
everyone inside will expire.

Scales, an Abecedarian Poem

All good boys do fine.
Believe me, I tried to
cooperate, memorizing
daily the order of notes
every hour, minute, and second.

For months, I pressed keys —
going up and down the scale but
having no ear for sound intricacies,
it was no easy task for me.
July arrived; my legs grew antsy for
kicking balls around the field, chasing
lightning bugs, capturing the on-off flash.

My mother yelled, *Practice! Practice!*
No play until you play
over and over again. I
prayed for broken keys,
quizzes arriving in fall with the
return to school, for
summer's long hours to cease.
To end my rolling excuses in the music room.

Understanding my lack of talent, I wanted to
veer away from this instrument
world. Banging my hand, I wished for
x-ray proof of damage
yearning only this—to never play a
zippy version of "Yankee Doodle" again.

Splatter

Driving on macadam in darkness,
we strive to avoid
sprinting deer, scampering squirrels.

Does it matter that our intent
is innocent—to arrive
safely at a spot on a map?

We, too, are just animals
darting across dark roads
after dusk descends,

shunning infliction
on the bodies of others,
failing in the end.

Line Dancers

Conformists, they prefer

line dances—the Cupid Shuffle,

the Cha Cha Slide, the Wobble.

These are the workers

who follow, don't lead,

who merge with the pack,

timid part of the audience

who clap, two hands

raised, one small section

of the giant stadium wave.

Indecisive

They are always in front
of me at coffee shops,
squinting at overhead
menu boards as if trying
to solve for X.

X is frappuccino or black coffee
or cappuccino or pour-over brew
or maybe tea for a change
or, *What is the special of the day
and what do you recommend?*

Finally, with equation solved,
the customer digs around
in her purse for bills and change,
bank or gift card,

or another patron left his wallet
in the car. *Can you just wait
a few minutes while I run out
to retrieve it?* By then,

my blood pressure has risen
into the danger zone. I've
ground my front teeth to nubs
and mouthed eight curses and
one *come on already*.
When it's finally my turn—
I've forgotten the order completely.

Aisle

She knows this will end
but sees the seated
wedding guests dressed
and waiting. Beyond the temple
windows are three unborn sons
wanting to emerge from the future.

She looks down
at her white satin-
covered feet that do not
want to budge forward,
but faces stare back.
The chuppah appears
like a garden door.

The man in a tuxedo stands
at his mark on the stage,
empty spot beside him.
She feels his prodding eyes,
three sons
beckoning her forward.

Grocery Lines

I have a knack for picking
the wrong grocery line,
the same one that moves
speedily until my arrival.

The register tape
runs out, a bakery item
is missing the UPC code,
the older woman in line only writes
checks and takes five minutes
to fill out said check,
another five minutes to find
her license.

Then the coupon lady can't
locate a certain coupon,
leaves slowly to search
aisle five before returning,
then as a lawyer
defends a client's life
in court, she proceeds
to argue the small print

on the coupon to allow usage.

Next, the system goes down,
reboots just in time for another
customer to challenge
a mismarked chicken package.

Finally, the *Register Open* light flicks off,
the belt stops moving,
the cashier shakes
her head and announces, *Break*.

Basho, Spring, and My Shadow

Basho waits for me,
sits gently on the desk
in that calm pink-petal manner,
his lines still
speaking of sparrows
and flowers all morning long.

Spring again, I want to watch
daffodils opening in the yard,

but my restless legs fidget,
wiggle with longing for roads
and travel. This potent gene of motion
runs through my red-vein river.

I need to walk forward,
keep moving away from
my own sinking shadow
that pulls me down on this dirt-
grounded, wooden stake
of place, but the child
inside keeps running away.

Why Worry

The logging truck
rumbling in front of me,
bungees flapping free,
heading south at eighty.
Wood threatening
decapitation, amputation.

Sometimes, jet plane
wheels and engines
drop from the heavens
crushing vans and cars.

Hot air balloons swoon
into power lines,
passengers toppling
onto roads and vehicles.

No wonder my eye twitches
and my heart leaps
every time I depart
the safety of my front door.

OPPOSITION

Fire Sale, Baby

Welcome to the fire sale, Baby.
The Devil opened his mouth
and breathed on my house.

I'm disposing of every last thing —
Queen Anne mahogany chairs, end
tables, the fiddle, the violin.

But I'm keeping all my sins —
philandry, gluttony, envy,
and sloth. Come on in, take

the gold-rimmed Lenox china,
the ivory-tusk chandelier. Burn
until all ceilings and floors are bare.

The Devil's waiting for me
to join him on the happy hour
tour. We'll pound down gin

while we sing the last adagio
and dirge, watch the flames blow out
the roof, purge the last tchotchke.

Terrible Dictators

Sometimes, a giant rooster
takes over the mountain.

Call him animal, call him
dictator; both labels fit.

The squawking is the same;
it leads to a common endgame.

Years later, when guns are locked
away, nameless corpses rise.

A rooster hides behind every hill;
weak ears wander, then follow him.

The Arbitration

is non-binding but necessary.
Only one party shows up.
The defendant said he would
but sends a lawyer instead.
He is so clever—changing
the dance steps before the dance.

No one is cross-examined.
The plaintiff reads from the agreement.
The other side moves words
around, pretends one thing
means another. The wordsmith
laughs. The other side says,
One plus one equals cow.

The plaintiff says, *Two. It's two!*
Everyone knows it's two.
The lawyers collect their fees.
The plaintiff leaves, crazed,
yelling, *Two, not cow!*

Making My Students Cry in Class

Tears are not the expected outcome
of the brainstorming lesson I assign
in class. I guide them: list life events,
then select the one that pulls you in—
that hurricane eye capable of devouring.

After a five-minute free-write session,
I call on a first-row girl randomly.
She says, *At six, I lost my house.*
I picture foreclosure, eviction.
My house burned down. She adds,
Two sisters nearly died. Tears then
flood her face, drip on the desk.

I hold up my hand, say, *Stop. You can
stop.* But it's too late. Floodgate now
opened. I've summoned the heat
into this classroom, the sounds
of screaming children, scent of singed
hair rising. *I'm sorry*, I say.

But now the entire classroom is burning
down, the walls flaming away, her tears
soaking the floor. I have nothing
to offer, not even a tissue to douse
the nose and tears. On day one I said,

Words matter, explaining how
they can conjure up worlds
to escape to, but even I forgot the lesson
I once knew: sometimes words open up doors
that were meant to stay forever closed.

The Squirrel Trapped in the Ceiling of the Adjunct Office

Sound of thumping against the ceiling grate
disrupts my essay-grading momentum in the adjunct
office at the college. I wait, look up, search
for a bright-hued helium balloon stuck between two floors.
Thump, thump, thump continues to prevent
my paper grading. Who could concentrate
with all this noise? I stare at square-poised
holes in the ceiling cover and discover a gray
tail swishing back and forth. A squirrel blur
reveals itself. Yes, I do recall the phrase
open door policy when applying for this position;
every being has the right to learn. But now,
just like me, he is stuck here in a place
without benefits. Trapped between walls. No acorn
to chew, no water to relieve his thirst.
Couldn't he have chosen a more lucrative
office? My own son recently said
if I taught chemistry or math, I'd be
full-time and employable. I shake my head,
listen as the squirrel, too, resigns himself to stagnation.
Soon he'll starve or just give up. Humanity and humanities

silenced in darkness between two floors.
I return to the task at hand—grading papers
scribbled by the future generation, my stomach growling
for lunch I cannot afford, the hem of my gray pants
unraveling.

It's Good to Get Lost

So what if you end up in Tennessee
when North Carolina was your destination.
Get lost in the mountains frequently.

View the snaking creek, the sunset
and dusk. Sometimes you meet strangers
this way—husbands and lovers, too.

So if your GPS goes haywire
on your way home
from Cherokee, take it as a sign.

Splendid accidents happen
when you need them to.
Put away the maps. Wander
the mountains compass-less.

Bend

Stars and ocean
move away. Old lovers
and sand, too.

I tie rope to objects,
attempt to keep trees
and flowers near.

But when I close this
body off to you,
all falls away.

The lettuce wilts,
branches break,
feathers flee.

I lean this body
toward the living,
try to stay near

where we have been.
There is no truth here
but this vanishing.

Casting Away Sins

I am done casting sins
into that good river.
This loaf of bread
is too luscious to toss
away to the ducks and fish.

You say
cleansing is necessary,
like a baptism of flesh.

Who are you to designate
the good and the bad?
Demolish your own bed
of flowers with words.

Remember how Hansel
and Gretel left a trail
of crumbs in the forest?
Hungry animals will eat away
the only known path home.

Meteorology

Even the weather doesn't know
what it wants to become;
winter attempts to yield
to spring, then back-steps
to the dance of deeper freeze.
Thundersnow drums in the field.

Heavy sweaters sway against
short sleeve t-shirts in the closet.
While velvet pants suffocate tennis skirts,
sandals step on suede boots in defiance.

Gray squirrels remove
their careful stashes, only to return
nuts to their winter rooms.

How can we know where to go
or what to become when highs
and lows dervish dance around town?
Heat flashes loom, pollen disperses,
then a Nor'easter arrives after Easter.

Snow coats grass and flower petals,
killing what transiently blooms.

When the Devil Comes Knocking

I answered the door at midnight
when I heard the devil
knocking. I was lonely.
Can you blame me for answering?

He carried a noose inside his sordid bag
of props and trickery. I invited him in.
How does one recognize the devil?
There were no horns, no red skin.
His handshake felt the same as human.

He made promises: *I'll rescue you
from the storm. I'll take you to the Bahamas—
all warm breezes and palm trees, with turtles
that crawl up the hot sand. No blizzards
will ever block the roads again.*

I believed him. He hung a gold circle
on the ceiling; it dangled like the moon
hollowed out. *Set your lovely pale neck
inside the emptiness.*

Then the wind suddenly blew in,
knocking down the ring. His mask blew off
revealing red fire, and horns popped up upon
his sharp head. *It's what you wanted!*
Don't think me bad or wrong.

Storms have a way of clearing
what does not belong. The moon
not hollowed out appeared outside.
And the only other circle visible—
my lips opening to release that one defiant word.

Reveal

Let's rendezvous in the neighborhood
of questions. Half of all conversation
carries the weight of speculation
about previous stations of recreation,
such as the locations of stomping grounds
and specific companions including
a long list of past lovers and acquaintances.

Isn't the goal to set fresh fires
to the yard's sod of conversation?
To reach the shunned pause-point of hesitation,
that seesaw teetering and rising
before the downward push and bump?
To reveal a flush in the cheeks, averted
eyes and such? Don't merely arrive under
the auspices of polite etiquette.

You and I both know that's all just dustcover
and plastic-wrap preservation for couches.
The desire still exists to romp upon manners

and grandmother's shielded upholstered furniture.
Raise a wildfire beneath flimsy surfaces;
startle us with those towers you once built
inside the golden city of your halcyon days.

Migraines Ashore in Florida

When I saw the headline,
I wondered why migraines floated
ashore. I pondered images —
fish huddling in a wet scrimmage.
I wanted to know what vehicle
carried this menace to the southern
boot-tip. Was it delivered by small vessel
or by ship, canoe or other flotsam?
Or was it conveyed by a single fish,
released in one bubble from his lips?
What swimming thing beneath the warm Gulf waves
was messenger to pain? Stingray
or Portuguese man o' war,
attaching jellied tentacles to abdomen
or head, injecting that dreaded throbbing
to a bobbing or flailing extremity.

> Mine are triggered by stress, chocolate,
> red wine, hormonal fluctuations during that certain
> time of month. It started when I lived out West.
> First, I lost peripheral vision. My strength was tested
> for days as I rested, filled with pain in a lightless room.

The nausea, vomiting, sharp stone pressed against
my sanity, would not fade fast enough for me.

But why migraines in Florida? Were they attracted
to oranges, mangroves, alligators, palm trees?
What was the tidal pull? I looked again, my head throbbing
with questions. I laughed at my mistake after
rearranging letters properly on the page and saw
that in fact it read, *Migrants Ashore in Florida.*
It said that two hundred Haitians jumped overboard,
swam or waded ashore to ensure a proper future.
They fled from the poorest country to be denied
asylum here. Shown in newsprint like black on white
    concrete,
like letters set all wrong on a page, letters that must
be rearranged, turned around in the end to get it right.

Food Fight at Walmart

Wouldn't Ginsberg be disturbed today
watching a shootout in the produce
section of the local Walmart?
While the old grubber looked on,
the outlaws desiccated tomatoes, avocados,
and eventually flesh, body parts
(non-organic and organic the same price here),
wrangling about my banana and your orange,
about taking and getting and mine and yours.
Couldn't one of the men take a bite
out of crime or a Granny Smith instead,
wander forward, push the grocery cart
through the Muzak-filled aisles? Just walk away.
Forget the Wild West machismo and leave
that damn cart, the guns and the bullets, in the corral.

Curmudgeons

We have become them —
intolerant of toddler ramblings
and rages in coffee stations,
their yawping over burgers
and corndogs in restaurants.
We who once expected adoration
for our loins' creations
now ask for a table location
very far away from them.

Circle on Canvas

You say the inkblot
spot on canvas is just ink;
you do not think circles
against white have
essential meaning.

Look at the pupil
in my eye, dear student,
or the wide round
of my open mouth.

See how when I scream
from this lip-circle,
the family in the house
fire survives.

The Angry Son Grows Up

Denied entry at the elite academy,
he rolls dice and clichés disperse:
God is dead and there never was
a God and the universe is made
of random dots on a die and
there is no grand plan and
why did you teach me about
honesty and fairness and truth
instead of corruption and lies?
At least then I'd know how to
play their tainted games to win.

Folly

The once-enthusiastic lover has left
the building, couple-hood euthanized
for single-status, post-romance mortem.
Amused now and in cahoots with another woman,
he exchanges the keys of the marriage house
for cohabitation with his new relation.

The judge will not recuse him from responsibility;
it is not enough to grab car keys and shoes, then
turn away from that other used-up life. Beware
of men who leave a wife without hesitation.

Watch out for his new muse's extracurriculars—
singing the blues in a late-night bar where
some other Romeo dude is watching, waiting for
a midnight roll and ruse. What's good for him
is good for her, too. All just fodder and subterfuge.

The Ant

How easy to be
the ant on concrete
scrambling toward
the apple slice
for sustenance.

Driven by need,
the ant joins
the worker community
to satisfy hunger.

What of disparate
forms of desire?
Two birds mingling,
merging mid-flight.

New lovers necking
against the sedan.
The quenching of thirst
after the marathon ends.
What comes later

when our bellies are filled,
all desire of need
and want depleted?
Does the ant wander lost
and alone in the forest?

Education

Consent to hip-hop rigor,
then watch educators balance
cultural references
with textbook rhetoric.

The boon times of pumping
up egos has waned;
now, cocky teens know
less than little.

They hold their growing
chins high anyway,
expecting trophies
for effort and plump
bank accounts
in exchange for lethargy
and lazy days.

The hungry hum
of technology

swallows classroom funds
and direction while
classic literature

waits untouched
in library tombs,
the pages aching for
distant fingers
to turn their lonely pages.

TALES FROM THE CITY

My Father Returns from New York City

My father murmured in a hushed voice
(my ears overheard down the hall)
in an index-finger-over-the-lips shushed
kind of tone, *I hit a girl today,*

as if the wind had stirred between city
buildings, propelling abandoned, discarded
printed papers forward, damaged stories
flying across the streets and avenues.

He whispered to my mother, his voice
thick, tripping with liquor, *A bad girl.*
I hit a bad girl today with my car
(in a city lined with poverty, prostitutes).

These words—as if small birds burst forth
from the nest, wings extended, and could not
fly. My father had once said to me
when the baby bird fell broken-winged

from the tree to the overgrown summer grass,
his lips so close to my face my cheek warmed,
We cannot save her. And I watched that
last breath push from her feathered chest.

At 6 AM You Still Speak with Your Father

Now you pass your father
in the hall, expecting an answer
to slink out of him. He is
hung, framed. Dead.

He stares back at you
in black and white, the outline
of his mouth (your mouth) still
holding its disapproval.

It is morning, when your brain
has yet to wake, and you hear
his deep voice in the hallway
calling, *Maureen, Maureen.*

Sometimes in dreams he speaks
too, continuing those
winding-maze arguments
that never find an answer out.

God Whispers

At night God whispers,
Hold on, and she runs
her hand over

the chalky scar on her lip.
The pillow unzippers
and her dreams spill

from the bed.
Every dream has been
marred by that first injury.

Jazz Club Limbo

Anything can happen on this island—
cheaters continue to cheat, wives
throw up their arms and leave.
Yellow lights turn green.

At the jazz club, you bump
into a slew of old friends;
they slip warnings inside
your pocket with a wink.

One friend says she's now
stuck living in a house
with a man she's grown
to hate. A dud, a slug.

There's the one who married
too quickly and now cannot
leave. She lifts her sleeve
to reveal a bruise, whispers, *Lose*.

Foreshadowing crawls in syncopation
thick in the black-walled room.

Still, hopeful trumpet notes blare,
the bass sends scales up and down

with flare. Strings tug at
your all-over-the-place emotions.
A line appears outside the door.
One stiletto heel remains inside,

the other one outside. The moon
asks the question again,
Why fear this forward motion?
Never one to burn the bridge,

you know you'd rather jump
and risk your future.
You slowly contemplate
the black street ahead,

distance that cannot be seen; yet
you see far enough to know answers.
So you hover there, one foot inside
the club, waiting through

an upbeat song, twirling
into another dance with
yourself. Sometimes decisions
are made by not making them.

Gate

Sit still, child. Listen:
the creaking gate
opens and closes.

It's vital to know
who comes and who
goes. That's why

the old woman sits
by the window and watches
from sunrise till dusk.

Happy Hour

Happy Hour arrives again.
Music trumpets on, notes release
into the bar air, first an adagio,
then sixties elevator folk tunes. A man
slumps bar-seat low in ruins, downs
four bourbons in a row and some carpaccio.

You dive inside your own
cabernet, five bucks this time
of day, from six till seven. Burgundy
heaven in a flute. It suits
you well. You swish it side
to side within the glass, a residue
resides then slides away.

This is not named Sad Folks
Hour, yet every loner
at the bar wears that
end-of-work-day frown,
eyes turned down and then away.

An older man flashes blue eyes
and a smile, but then his stare
returns to the comfort of
the hovering television screen safely
displaying baseball, where a pitcher
throws a curveball to a batter
standing at the plate.
The player slams the ball far into
the sky as if it really matters.
As if anything really matters.

Barstool Time

It's lemon-drop martinis
all sugar-rimmed liquor

on our tongues, sipping
from frosty beer mugs

while we hum old tunes
from our high barstools

mouthing happy hour
chitter chatter. We scatter

here for music and appetizer
fare to share the day's stories

amid these glorious empty
nest years, not wanting

ever to leave
these wooden chairs.

Change of Address

You've relocated to this plot
of land; a plaque is placed
to display the new address.

"Born" and "Died" are cross
street names. Years indicate
time spent on this
map of time. They've even set

a bench right here
for guests to stop and stare,
digress, ramble on
with greetings and regrets.

Smoke

Plunked down in the desert,
an adult playground of neon lights,
performers, and games
where I went to play cards, drop coins
inside ringing machines, watch
acrobats fly across carnival air
while magicians onstage made
people disappear then reappear.
Beyond the tent, sun and land
created their own natural mirages.

Once, on arrival, my plane circled
for hours above smoke that drifted in
from Los Angeles forest fires.
When I stepped into the heated air,
I choked, wandered, lost and confused
by the onslaught of fuzzy flashing lights.
Vegas, where nothing and everything
seemed dreamlike, where anything
could happen. And here we are
again. Smoke now from a gun,
the people trapped in wildfire,

unable to escape from this valley's mirage, caught between life and death.

Those Who Do Sickness

Eighty-year-olds never sick
in life except for
the common cold
do sickness poorly,
fill exam rooms
with complaints, kvetch
about midnight wake-ups
for pressure checks and meds.
Release day elicits cheers
from the staff. As each nurse
and orderly murmur,
*Do not let the door hit you
on the way out,* they pull
off their gloves, glad
to be rid of wimpy whiners.

Sick people learn how
to do illness well —
for hospital visits
they pack warm pajamas,
books, and magazines.
They don't wince at

the needle prick.
Lab techs are seen
as happy visitors,
little helpers on the road
to wellness. Patients
transform to jolly comediennes.

My Neighbor Cleans Up Crime Scenes

Picture the aftermath of murder.
Measure the distance
from body to bloodstains. Trace
the splatter of scattered droplets,
the red path from the murderer's shoes.
Inhale the imagined stench of death. Wonder
which cleaners and tools are used
to wipe away anger and violence.
Do death stains ever really fade?

He says there is schooling for specifics —
like clothing to wear to protect his own skin.
What about his interior, unsuited self?
Does he dream of swimming slowly
through red seas? Does he hear voices,
the victims' last words? When he listens
to angry voices rising in other rooms,
does he shake his head? Once so intimately
familiar with what human hands can do,
does he stare at his own palms
in the moonlight and ask, *Why? How? When?*

Bubble Yum Urban Myth

We thought for sure spider eggs
waited to sprout from the gum.

We pictured baby spiders crawling
down our tongues into our lungs.

In the morning, I would open my mouth
to respond to my mother's scolding

and out they would march, the answer
to a thousand unspoken questions.

Lips

When her lips were just lips,
depository for questions and phrases
where sentences departed
before another set of lips
discovered hers,
she watched giant faces merging
on big screens as space between
two famous actors vanished.

She'd never witnessed
her own parents engaging
in this affection exhibition.
At ten, she practiced
with a pillow while her parents
argued down dim halls.

Finally, one summer
at the first boy-girl party,
the Australian exchange
student invited
her into that dark room.

His accent vanished.
The air between them receded;
she felt his lips on hers,
the exchange of tongues.
When their faces parted,
her entire universe had shifted.

The Worker

She labors until her body buckles.
What choice is there?
Blisters homestead on swollen feet.
The world is cruel this way.

Work owns most waking hours,
but one lifted minute of indulgence
beneath the stars can sustain
her for a thousand shifts.

Wealthy People

Beside an ocean
a mansion burns down.

Remains of four children
wait to be revealed.

Money is no deterrent to fire.
Death is blind to gold-lined pockets.

Deals are not made beyond
the ethereal boardroom.

The wisest parents always keep
one eye open in search of flames.

At the Greyhound Bus Station, Nashville

In Tennessee, my son wanders away
from the bus station, ends up
in a seedy section of Nashville.

Oblivious one, he does not notice
the shady man, the needles in the street,
broken windows, graffiti, dangling gutters.

Boy who sees only birds and sky,
the gaggle of geese marching forward,
not the gangbanger suddenly beside him

or that he's ended up near a warehouse.
The hoodlum robs his wallet of cash,
credit cards, license—his body of trust.

And of course, this, too, is my fault,
not teaching him street smarts.
Raised in Jersey, it flows through my veins.

But my child, whom I shielded
from weed-grown tracks and alleys,
wanders there without me

and doesn't know how to get back.

About the Author

Maureen Sherbondy's poems have appeared in *Prelude, Calyx, European Judaism, The Oakland Review,* and other journals. She has won the Hart Crane Memorial Poetry Contest, the North Carolina Poet Laureate prize, and many other awards. Her most recent poetry books are *Dancing with Dali, The Art of Departure,* and *Eulogy for an Imperfect Man.* Sherbondy teaches English at Alamance Community College in Graham, North Carolina.

About the Press

Unsolicited Press was founded in 2012 and is based in Portland, Oregon. The press produces stellar fiction, nonfiction, and poetry from award-winning writers. Authors include John W. Bateman, T.K. Lee, Rosalia Scalia, and Brook Bhagat.

Find the press on Twitter and Instagram: @unsolicitedp

Learn more at www.unsolicitedpress.com.

www.ingramcontent.com/pod-product-compliance
Lightning Source LLC
Chambersburg PA
CBHW021448070526
44577CB00002B/317